MOON WALK

*A poetic walk on
the self-exploration
of darkness
and light*

ELIZABETH DUNCAN

Copyright © 2023 by Elizabeth Duncan

All rights reserved.

No part of this book may be reproduced in any manner whatsoever except in the case of brief quotations embodied in critical articles and reviews.

The information in this book is true and complete to the best of the author's knowledge. Any advice or recommendations are made without guarantee on the part of the author. The author disclaims any liability in connection with the use of this information. The ideas, suggestions, and procedures provided in this book are not intended as a substitute for seeking professional guidance.

Library of Congress Control Number (LCCN)
2023919308

ISBN Number
9798218297046

Cover and Interior Design by Katarina @nskvsky

Printed in the United States of America

To my love, my husband.

To those who pick up this book, thank you for giving my words a chance.

To me, for the audacity to dream and the courage to pursue those dreams.

CONTENTS

BETRAYED - LOYAL	3, 4
FAMILY UNDEFINED - FAMILY DEFINED	5, 6
LONELY, SCARED TO TRY - RELENTLESS, FEARLESS	7, 8
ORDINARY, MEDIOCRE - EXIST BIG	9, 10
SAFER IN SILENCE - DISCOVER MY VOICE	11, 12
FAILURE - NEW ATTEMPT	13, 14
A SNAKE, A FAKE - FRIEND	15, 16
REPEATED LESSONS - LESSON UNDERSTOOD	17, 18
OPPOSITION - CONTENT	19, 20
SOFT, WEAK - BRAVE, STRONG	21, 22
WANDERLOST - PURPOSE FULL	23, 24
SUICIDE - STAY	25, 26
TRAUMA - HEALING, HEALED	27, 28
WHAT PEOPLE THINK OF ME - WHAT I THINK OF ME	29, 30
NO GRATITUDE, NO RECOGNITION - DO GOOD ANYWAY	31, 32
A LIE - THE TRUTH	33, 34
VILLIAN - HERO, HERO IN	35, 36

CONTENTS

TEMPTATION, TEMPTATION WON - SACRIFICE	37, 38
REACTIVE - DISREGARD, IGNORE, DISMISS	39, 40
IGNORANT, RACISM & HATE - APPETITE FOR KNOWLEDGE	41, 42
NON-BELIEVER, WHY GOD - GOD'S LOVE, JESUS	43, 44
PAST - FUTURE	45, 46
INFATUATE - LOVE	47, 48
PHASES OF IMMATURITY - MATURING	49, 50
ABUSED - ESCAPE	51, 52
STUBBORN - COMPLIANT, LET GO	53, 54
DRUG ADDICTION, FALL APART ADDICTIONS COME BACK TOGETHER, REFORM	55, 56
LOCKED UP, PRISON - FREE, FREED	57, 58
ASSUME - CERTAINTY	59, 60
GRIEF, LOSS - THE PAIN	61, 62
PERFECTION - NOT PERFECT, AUTHENTIC	63, 64
GOLIATH - DAVID	65, 66
COCKY - CONFIDENT	67, 68
~ AND ~ THE DUALITIES	70
DEPRESSED - LAUGHTER	71, 72
EMPTY - HAVE IT ALL TOGETHER	73, 74

CONTENTS

FOLLOWER – LEADER	75, 76
NO – NO	77, 78
TRAUMA – PROGRESS	79, 80
MIND – HEART	81, 82
CONFUSED – GRATEFUL	83, 84
STEM – ARTS	85, 86
DIFFERENT, BY SOCIETY – I AM, I'M	87, 88
NIGHT – MOON	89, 90
ACKNOWLEDGEMENTS	92

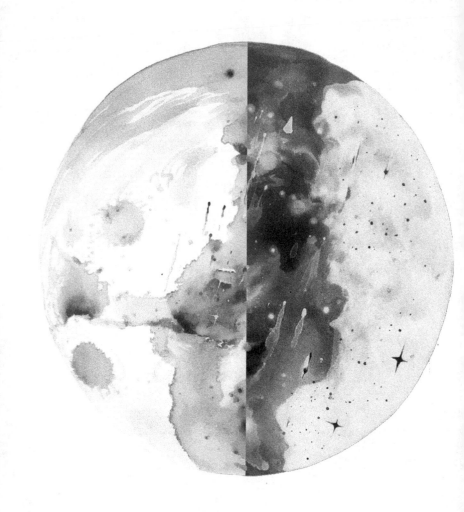

author's note

Writing is how I explore and reason complex equations of the mind and heart. As a child I knew I'd found my moral connection, to help others by expression. Whether it's observations in my point of view, my personal experiences, or exposing half-truths, writing chose me.

As a resiliency instructor in the military, I understood and advised those I taught that the only way to reclaim your power after a tough challenge was to adjust your mental flexibility and look for the meaningful opportunity. In other words, find the light.

Moon Walk is formatted with our dark experiences, thoughts, and behaviors on the *left side* of the page and our light self-talk on the *right side* of the page, representing our conscience (the devil and angel) in action. When you find yourself in dark situations, dangerous to your potential, can you find the light?

I've read many books throughout my life and what sticks out to me the most is the need for practical ways to approach mental and emotional battles. A few biblical examples are: *what were Daniel thoughts in the lion's den or how did Joseph mentally overcome the betrayal of being sold by his brothers or the anger in Cain towards Abel when his offering was rejected?*

Moon Walk is lyric poetry from the dark side and the light side of the battlefield, our mind. The moon represents the light within us, while the night represents the darkness. This is my reconnaissance of "choices."

It was important to manifest that *choosing* a light mindset *will* illuminate the darkest of experiences. Nevertheless, we're responsible for not allowing toxic tendencies to outweigh the positive in you.

You'll feel heard, encouraged, seen, and responsive. I'm impassioned for you to use this book…as a written flashlight so to speak. Find the opportunities to challenge your perspectives and use light to somersault the hurdles thrown your way because our mindset matters.

Elizabeth Duncan

Betrayed

Once upon a time
I thought it was safe
to bring you
into my world.
Trust you with
me, time, money.
You got me.
Shame on me.
When you weighed your options
it was worth losing me.
can't be.
The signs are always signaling.
Ole hopeful optimistic me.
In most situations
people make the obvious choice.
themselves.
It's not only selfish, it's regular.
a mediocre frequency.
the devil playing you
but in time you'll see
you played yourself
playing me.
In a world of
empty words,
I got completely carried away.
Now the mask is off
this is the real you
revealed.

Realistically, betrayal happens. It comes in the form of manipulation, insincerity, and other duplicitous behavior. Betrayal can also redirect. That revelation was dire to your survival. Don't ignore the inconsistences, the energy shifts, or the indirect signs. Pay attention to the roaring silence.

Loyal

A loyal intent is
not perfect.
it's year after year of
support in your absence.
Discovering actions
that are parallel to words.
I'll never be
flawless nor will you.
I'll expect
difference of opinions
right and wrong choices
distance and broken hearts
wounds that leave scars
but what will it reveal?
you're still genuine.
A good vulnerability.
A space to expose pain.
Impartial and tender.
Tough and receptive.
Corrective and safe.
This is rare.
I feel extremely blessed.
I give you a bouquet
of gratitude.
You bring an authentic
connection.
You have my automatic
reciprocation.
Relationship.
Real.
definitions
revealed.

Family - Undefined

Unchosen bonds,
watering my foundation.
Related by blood,
a cultural representation.
I'm fascinated by
physical similarities.
Ancestorial veins flowing
from heart to heart.
Understanding the family
generational light and dark.
Just because they're near,
is all family dear?
I'm an orphan,
my family disappeared.
I'm adopted,
my family tree has grafted.
I don't have a biological family.
minus the hesitation,
I'm rooted in the *idea*
of family.
Trusting people placed before me.
I respect the ancestry of me.
I've accepted the loose bonds
estranged relationships
deep rooted conflicts
disguised agendas
empty greetings
but the family foundation was set.
For clarity,
family doesn't make you *family*.
I read about Cain and Abel.
Family associates.
Family is human.

Family - Defined

It feels good
to belong
to matter
to fellowship with your people.
In mutual support laughter
and encouragement.
Passing through storms safely.
Crying together.
Covering me with words of
affirmation and
praying for each other's
well-being.
Creating the family description,
an unconditional lineage.
A cultural tradition
of like and love.
Family is a compilation
of nurtured relationships
years of floods and blood
over years of understanding.
Family is deserving
unsuspecting friends.
Humans who breathe life
into you time and time again.
Leaving lots of room
for a tender approach
soft patience
forgiveness and
bricks of hope.
A foundation was set.
but it takes years of intent.
Building genuine connections.
Wishing well despite holes
of darkness.
Longing for family to measure
the manuscript above.
I co-created my family tree
and it's still all love.

Lonely - Scared to Try

Saying it is one thing,
the realization of doing it
brings me up breathless.
bet on me...this me?
I don't like to bet because
I don't like to lose.
Every day is a constant fight
in my mind.
Why would I subject myself
to the unknown?
big dummy.
either you're really determined
or a psycho.
The worry is overwhelming.
The what ifs are smothering.
Is there someone to call
when you feel scared?
I would never admit that
without feeling weak.
At this rate,
I can talk myself out of it.
a consistent voice of self-doubt.
That's what it'll take.
A dangerous disbelief of never succeeding.
My next move will be lonely and scared.
I can't do it.

Beginning anything challenging is a mental shock. Be mindful of what you allow into your orbit and what you say to yourself. The more you think about the process - what it takes to start - the more frequent your bowel movements. Seriously. It's not easy to take off the dangers of uncertainty. However, it's pivotal to face the direction of your goals and see the finish line.

Relentless - Fearless

think, plan, execute.
Take your chance
and
do it scared.
The flex is,
I don't need
a coping mechanism.
I need faith.
On the ground,
I performed with enthusiasm.
In the sky,
I discovered my wings.
I'm not impressed
with difficulty.
I am pressed on:
how bad do I want it.
When I start to *deny* my talent,
call me "Relentless."
I'm connected to a
deranged determination.
When I start to *doubt* my talent,
call me "Fearless."
I'll reassure the dark
it's the light in me.
I'll be willing to risk
everything.
a wild card.
Reverse fear with
persistence.
This accomplishment
is my fearless
exhibition.

Ordinary - Mediocre

I'd rather blend in.
dumb it down a little.
I'll go through life using
my brokenness
my anger
as an anchor.
uninspired.
I'll exist in
the confusion
of my significance.
I'll hold in my curiosity.
I'll dress quiet.
I don't want to appear
extra
or offend the normal.
The bare minimum
is enough.
bland is the aesthetic.
I just want to fit in
with everybody else.
My effort is lackluster.
average is better than
below.
I won't entertain the idea
of challenging myself
to be great.
What if I'm meant to be inferior.
I'm okay with that.

Oh, the possibilities to soar. You are a one-of-a-kind supernatural magical spirit human being. I believe God would agree. Be your authentic self. Light your vivacious flame. You are INSPIRATION.

Exist Big

I was given flare.
An incredible mind
and
a fascinating soul.
I won't hold back.
My high spirit is
my best self.
I'll show up
authentically me
also known as
doing too much
unapologetically.
I don't regret
my uniqueness.
I'll be seen
complete.
I'll compete
with only
pleasing me.
I don't fit in.
I exist BIG.
effervescent.
charismatic.
effortless
confidence.
I stand out.
Taking up the space
carved out
just for me.

Safer in Silence

I've never felt
completely safe.
Someone to fight for me.
at least listen to me.
What will happen
if I say something?
I've never done
this before.
This secret
took a big chunk of
my self-esteem.
I'll just tuck it away.
Silence feels safer.
It's my fault.
My voice won't matter.
Okay, today is the day.
I will tell someone close.
See! Nothing happened!
Life is all about
secrets, huh.
Burying them
with deep insecurity.
silent inhales
suffering exhales.
From here on out
if something terrible happens
I'll get over it.
pile it on.
People are dealing with
their own problems.
what was I expecting?
them to care.
I'll manage my expectations.

Discover My Voice

I rediscovered my voice.
I won't give any power
to who hurt me.
I'll be assertive and
tell my story.
Does humanity
share in the silence?
Did shame keep me quiet?
There's fear of retaliation
but I'll honor my pain.
today.
You thought I wouldn't
speak out.
embarrassed, no.
authority, yes.
I'm setting others free.
I'll find someone
who will listen.
I have to fight for my story.
My bravery will make
a difference.
I'll stop blaming myself.
my heart is racing.
take deep breaths.
anxiety comes with healing.
say it out loud with conviction:
I'm honest and powerful.
I'm vulnerable and tenacious.
I'll scream my truth!
Can you hear me?
Look up,
I'm on the roof.

Failure

This is embarrassing.
I'll likely have to sell the house.
I thought this was a lucrative idea.
All my savings went to purchase
my food truck.
my down payment for a house.
I took a chance and
invested in myself.
I didn't pass my exam.
I didn't pass the bar.
I've been studying for months.
I'm such an idiot.
Why did I tell everyone about my new position!
now I'm laid off.
I played with everything I had,
and we still lost.
I didn't finish college.
What am I going to do with my life?
I choked during my presentation.
I thought I'd be married forever.
My credit score is terrible.
I'm in so much debt.
I'll never be a homeowner.
I can't pay my own bills.
I have a degree and
I can't find a job.
I'm a failure.

If it puts your mind at ease, we'll experience failure at some point in our lives. It's one of the two results of trying. We must give ourselves credit for each attempt, win or lose. Treat failure like you do success: embrace it and keep going.

A New Attempt

that loss
that setback
that "no"
taught me something.
I'm stronger than I seem.
My kids are watching me.
I'll inspire them
to keep trying
to keep applying
to keep praying
to work HARDER.
Yes, it's difficult.
Some days
I want to fold but,
this is my journey.
I'll work for myself one day.
I'm the head and
not the tail.
That job is mine!
I'll create a budget.
I'll hold myself accountable.
I will not lose again.
If I do,
failure only means
a new opportunity
a new attempt
to win
to study
to succeed.
I'm smarter than I thought.
My resilience is
my redemption.

A Snake – A Fake

It went wrong somewhere.
At some point, you decided.
am I really that naïve?
Or are you a great performer?
hmmm, not that great.
I attended a few jokes.
I saw the counterfeit in your eyes.
Your body language always spoke competition.
two questions:
when did your intent shift?
why wasn't there a conversation?
I think it's because you'd rather snake.
My first snake.
No shame. No kindness. No grace.
A taker, pharisaic, and cruel.
As I reread the memories
I realize it was difficult for you
to exist next to my light.
I'm not better than you
and you're not better than me.
In my *twisted* reality we could've discussed
what it meant to truly be human.
to express your dark and still be loved.
my only agenda was to maintain a real connection.
but it was premeditated.
this façade was all a lie.
I release the snake back on the ground.
My light is needed elsewhere.

People switch up in a blink of an eye. Trust what your eyes see by chance. Trust your instincts no matter the history. Friendships and relationships become illusions when battle tested. Sometimes, people choose dark. When we're in anger and hurt, it's hard to see past dark thoughts. Get past the unanswered questions and don't take anything personal. Accept that evil conquered their vision. Pray for them. Release them and get, out the way.

Friend

I have to guard
my loyalty
like I guard my heart.
when I'm around you
I sense energies
of a candid light
of devotion.
An environment that brings out
the softness in me.
If you don't agree or
if I make a mistake,
don't hold back.
Understand you never have
to pretend. Never.
uncomfortable conversations
is the clearest path friend.
How can we exist in
support and
disconnect from
envy or phoniness?
this is the tender risks of relationships.
What do you think about yourself?
What do you expect from this friendship?
Inevitably
life will change us.
We will see each other
for who we really are.
I hope we remain
genuine
protective
compassionate.
earned words.
I'll be here to remind you
to take care of yourself
first.
I no longer see the good.
I see the truth that
time will tell.

Repeated Lessons

I keep making the same mistakes.
Repeating the same lessons
as an adult.
what am I doing wrong?
I must be stubborn.
I definitely don't like
feeling angry
taken advantage of
or hurt.
or do I like the drama?
It might be a wise idea
to pay attention to
what I'm feeling.
even if I sacrifice
my heart.
when was the last time
I recalibrated my choices.
Reconsidered who I'm attracted to.
I need to identify
my self- sabotaging
behavior.
correct my thinking.
quit the insanity.
I'm uncapable of
making better decisions.
My grandmom even shared
her experiences.
My mom told me,
I don't listen.
Three times,
lesson still unlearned.
When will I take heed?

Lesson Understood

There's a chance
I don't interpret the lesson.
It's possible I don't take the advice.
I feel the gravitational pull
to wreck
to touch the fire
to feel the burn.
to see for myself.
I want to get it right
the first time.
I've heard,
"you'll learn the hard way."
I'm a student to
the teaching moment.
I'm learning to love me.
My next choice
will not lead to
heartbreak,
anger, or pain.
I'll listen.
I'm yearning to grow.
I'll pray for discernment.
I will not repeat the lesson.
Identical pain is unnecessary.
One time,
lesson learned.
understood.

Save yourself years of suffering by learning from other's mistakes. For example, using this book in the moment of finding the light. We can also learn from our own mistakes. Receive the lesson, love on what's broken, heal, then make the best decision for your life. It may take sacrifices but do what's necessary.

Opposition

When I smile
you don't smile back.
I go out my way
to be gracious and kind
but no matter what
you're bound and
determined
to dislike me.
The resistance
is loud.
repeatedly vicious.
it's so intentional
I look past you now.
talk to me about it.
even if you hiss.
You've assumed
my reaction
will cooperate
in the drama.
or confront you
with my observations.
nope.
I won't distort my character.
we're opposites.
What an honor it feels
to be opposed by
a light leech.
a stale spirit.
how exhausting it must be.
Your dark
is threatened.
It's a war for my peace.

It is so important, so *very, very* important to know who you are. When we're provoked by pessimists, complainers, and somber spirits, don't adapt to the toxicity. Your talent, your ideas, your light, YOU shine too bright in the dark.

Content

absolutely not
I will not cooperate.
Nope, to the
slightest sniff
of toxins.
Nope, to the
tiniest drop
of venom.
I see the hate.
I smell your bitter.
However,
God bless you.
let me very clear,
a piece of me is
tempted
to meet you
at the lowest level.
However,
my happiness
my mental health
is a priority.
This is my mature year.
I have control of
my mouth
my mood
my mind.
I won't take it personal.
I won't hold this
against you forever.
My hope is to inspire you
to show you
that you can
keep your light
in some of
the darkest hours.
I give you absolution.

Soft – Weak

Take it like a man.
crying inside,
unemotional faces outside.
Why is the suicide rate
higher for men?
coincidence.
I can't talk about my emotions.
I'm a G.
I have to be strong.
Real men don't cry.
I don't have emotions.
emotional aka soft.
Get over it.
I need tough skin.
I'll look like a victim.
nobody can see me like this.
instead, I'm angry.
No one will ever see me cry.
My father didn't cry.
I've had a hard life,
I don't cry.
I let everything get to me.
I can't handle it right now.
love makes me weak.
Man up.
I don't need help.

Who makes these one-size fits all rules? There's such a wide range of personalities walking this earth that challenge every cliché and every stereotype, especially for men. We have to let these ancient beliefs go, entertain better ways, and introduce new perspectives to define emotional intelligence. We're all-encompassing beings. We're able to regulate our emotions and still be strong.

Brave – Strong

I know who I am.
A Warrior.
A Human.
A Conqueror.
I'm not scared
to show my emotions.
I'm free
to release.
I'm not sorry
for being a victim.
This is the face
of courage.
I'm not ashamed
for choosing a safer path.
humans feel.
I can cry and
not be consumed
by sadness.
As a father,
I hug my son.
He'll recognize his anger
and know how to
manage sadness.
I acknowledge
my emotions
and move on.
love is a risk.
There is bravery
in emotional
communication.
There is courage.
in vulnerability.
Feel bravely.

Wanderlost

I'll go with the flow.
school not for everybody.
I'll figure it out as I go.
no serious plans.
There's no way I'll succeed
anyway.
You don't understand.
It takes
too much drive
too much faith.
too much focus.
I said I'll figure it out.
I don't have a purpose.
I'm not good at much.
It takes talent.
Setting goals I won't achieve.
I'm not even motivated.
I'd rather chill
get high and do me.
Don't worry about me.
I'm not smart like you.
My best is never
good enough.
I have no desire
right now
for hard work.
I'm satisfied doing nothing.

Do not deprive the world of your special gifts. You were made in God's great image, of course you have a purpose! Take the time you need to grasp it. You'll need to supply belief, effort, discipline, and hard work. Apply it, even if you feel hopeless. Encourage yourself to believe in your aspirations. It is imperative to believe in YOU.

Purpose Full

I decide today
I will not be defeated
by thoughts of
insignificance
complacency
or procrastination.
My dreams are worth
fighting for.
My purpose is the song
in my heart on repeat.
I hear a fighting voice
in my soul.
I trust in my abilities.
I defend my purpose
with passion and
resilience.
I'll fiercely try.
I will not be intimidated.
I'll find inspiration
to find my journey
to seek my full potential.
If I'm not motivated
to graduate
to list my goals
to believe in myself
to defy the odds
it will never happen.
My choices today design my future.
I'm committed to make every moment count.
Determination is crucial.
I'll find the possibilities.
This is my only story.

Suicide

I don't want to be here.
What does life want from me?
I don't want to live anymore.
Life is crushing me.
I'm tired of trying.
I'm tired of fighting.
If I end it today
then they'll miss me.
will they?
Maybe they'll see
how important I am
how serious I was.
Things have happened
I'll bring shame to my family.
There's only one way out.
No one sees me.
No one checks on me.
No one can fathom
my struggles.
They expect me
to get through this
on my own.
I'm pathetic.
I'm broke.
I'm a failure.
Existing is a struggle.
Everyone has turned their back on me.
God, it's getting real dark.
so dark you can't see me.
I'm at peace with my decision.
I hope I can convince you this is best.
You can't say I didn't try.
But I give up.
I want to commit suicide.

Stay

Somebody! Anybody!
Can you see me? *(yes)* *
hug me please. *(insert hug)* *
I just need somebody to listen.
I've been hiding in routine camouflage.
Can I sit here? *(yes)* * *(I care that you stay alive)* *
I'm glad you're here. *(I'm so happy you're here)* *
I'm happy I didn't give up.
I'll confront each day.
I'll fight the dark.
I'll fight these dark feelings.
God made me strong.
God made me.
I'm strong in every dilemma.
in every battle and every test.
I feel the darkness of pain.
I feel the darkness of anger.
It's bad.
It's hard to deal with right now.
I pray I can release it.
I gave it to God.
I'm important.
I feel seen.
I needed to talk it out.
Let me cry this out.
I see me now. I chose life.
Can you help me? *(yes)* *
(Let's go get some help.) *

* *This a dialogue.*

24/7 National Suicide Prevention and Crisis Lifeline # is 988.

Trauma

I'm constantly racially profiled.
My father doesn't know me.
My grandparents raised me.
I grew up in 4 different foster homes.
My mother's on drugs.
I've been raped.
I've had abortions.
I've been homeless.
I've been physically abused.
I've abused drugs.
I've seen things I can't repeat.
I've done things I wish I could forget.
It happened to me
and I didn't ask for it.
I'll never get past it.
The recruiter left out the nightmares.
I can't sleep.
If I had one word to describe the pain:
suffocating.
This can't be life.
Who would want me like this?
Who would hire a traumatized veteran?
I'd rather live in the shadows.
where you can't see the trauma.
operating in stress is all I know.
I exist in the dark.
The destiny of a nobody.
I have no fight to fight my issues.

You'll never meet a person who doesn't have a story. The lasting psychic effects of traumatic experiences can be overwhelming and difficult to overcome. You must entertain the facts: you CAN do it! You will get through. You are whole despite the circumstances of your story.

Healing- Healed

Feel it.
The pain is
teaching me something.
This is me.
At first,
healing feels like
an emotionally tiring
uncomfortable
confrontation.
Glory is in the suffering.
Stay locked in.
Fight is my mantra.
move past the past.
one step, next step.
Take a deep breath in.
Breathe out.
Grow.
Thrive in the midst of trauma.
Pain is power.
I'm more than qualified.
I'm worthy.
I speak light
to my broken spirit.
Prayer calms the negativity.
I can grow from mud.
I will pursue my dreams in spite of.
I will find my tribe and
face the moon.
This work is forever.
I've been *magic** all along

*magic ~ a power from within.

What People Think of Me

They* won't like me. I barely like me.
I peeped that but dam what did I do?
Maybe people can't analyze me.
You know what, if they don't reach out
I won't either. It feels one-sided.
Just talk regular.
No, I need to talk proper.
They must have heard something.
perceptions
sideline discussions
opinions
without me.
I can tell when the energy is off.
feels disingenuous.
I don't want an invite.
My post got 2 likes.
They talk bad about everybody.
except themselves.
I know they talk about me.
ugh, people are so draining.
I don't want to be left out.
Why do I feel obligated to be recognized or liked?

It's easy to lose yourself in a downward spiral of trying to gain approval or fit in. From today until forever, care *less* about what others think about you and care *a lot more* about what you think about yourself. Be kind to you. If you like it, great. If you don't like it, change it. You'll destroy your peace and your self-love depending on validation or attention from people. You are the only you that will ever walk this earth.

*they- them, the people with the opinion you sought after, the people you admire more than you.

What I Think of Me

I accept me.
My differences.
My flaws.
My awkward tendencies.
I'm the most beautiful
when I'm true.
When I show up as myself.
I release the need to
people please.
Their silence or rejection
is not the source
of my life.
My focus is
becoming a better me.
Peace is
loving who I am
every step of the way.
Above all, does Jesus like me?
I admit
I have a dope soul.
An irresistible character.
A light so bright.
I like me.
I'm committed to loving me.
Don't you dare doubt your worth.
Don't you dare doubt the beauty in the discomfort.
What if they don't like me?
What if I like me.

Some people will love you no matter what you do, and some people will never love you no matter what you do. Go where the love is.

No Gratitude - No Recognition

I don't mind
extending
serving
giving.
It's difficult now though.
I'm surrounded by takers.
Taking on additional duties,
working late to complete
the objective
sacrificing my personal time.
you're welcome.
It's normal around here
to operate in
no appreciation.
I hear,
"*Be the example*"
"*Be the bigger person*"
Eventually they'll realize
my worth.
maybe they won't.
I give and give and give.
I feel bad if I say no.
I've never received
a thank you
card or note.
I feel taken advantage of.
Givers need too.
I'm depleted and drained.
I literally have no light to give.
Should I reciprocate the energy?
or stop completely?
No one taught me
when to stop.

Do Good Anyway

Shout out to the givers.
Well done.
It feels good to go
above and beyond.
The reward of giving is
stimulating.
an extent of the heart.
I remember the why.
I'm content in my intent.
but I won't lose myself.
I won't be used.
I won't carry
resentment
waiting for gratitude.
I'll respect my time.
I'll give only
what I can offer.
I give myself permission
to stop.
now.
I have nothing to prove.
My character is naturally
kind.
It makes me exceptional.
I'm learning
the balance of
yes and no.
rather I'm used by God
serving as his angel.
Keeping the good in
goodness
gracious.

A Lie

There's motive.
a credulous influence in a lie.
Motivated at my demise.
to break me.
to hurt me.
the lie became
their truth.
and they believe it too.
I'm not going to pretend
it does bother me a little.
the covert passive aggressors.
I feel like the spectacle.
nice usually gets the disrespect.
Using my silence
as an easy target.
I feel betrayed God.
I want to be angry.
is this a lesson in disguise?
a test of faith?
can you shine your truth on me
so others can see?
the deceit is like an ex,
exposed.
I'm disappointed in the influence.
No one peeps the insufficiency.
Only the lies
they tale.
the devil is the lie.

Why shouldn't dark energies want to destroy you? If you look at it from a dark perspective, you'll realize there's no limit to harm you or damage your reputation. Unfortunately, we underestimate the power of deception. We never consider if the intention is to erase the love with hate. The substantial effects of lies are not spoken about frequent enough. I'll speak on it.

The Truth

I'm evidence.
I can handle
the lies
because
I am the truth.
Existing big.
The proof is in the pressure.
the truth:
spreads slower.
less appealing
to a crowd.
I'll remind my logic
of life's broken
and wild design.
This assignment
birthed
words with purpose.
a true demonstration.
The devil knows
my anointing
carries inspiration.
People will perform,
forgive them.
Life will be hard,
endure.
voluntary innuendo's,
give clarity.
I'll let people
believe
what they want.
It's literally out of
my control.
Remember whose you are.
I'm validated.
by truth.

Villain

This is the role
I chose to play.
the Scar.
the Ursula.
the Jafar.
I'd like to think
I didn't have a choice.
I'm the bad guy.
The one who marvels in destruction.
I inflict pain.
I harm the innocent.
I don't care.
I have no empathy.
I have an objective:
to steal, kill, and destroy.
It's your own fault.
You shouldn't trust everybody.
You should be careful who you love.
bet you learned a valuable lesson,
there's no benevolence
in evil.
I'll do whatever it takes.
only the strong survives.
Protect yourself.
I chose a side.
The villain role
was already written.

Disney movies display valuable life lessons of good versus evil. Take away the animation (but keep the songs), you'll find the world balances: givers and takers, peace and war, morals and demoralize, kind and mean, love and hate, and light and dark. It's bigger than a prince and princess. The divide is introduced.

Hero – Hero In

Good hearted
fair
trustworthy
words that exemplify the light.
I choose to set the bar.
a good bar.
This is not only
a safe space,
this is a
courageous space.
I care.
I still care.
to speak up.
to give.
to spread love.
to honor God.
our Hero
at night.
It's a dark world,
when it's corny
to do right.
Self-gain is
not my motive.
I see it differently:
I have a candle and
I'll light yours
with my flame.
I'll be the unusual.
I'd rather stand out anyway.
It would be a disservice
to my destiny
to not walk
confidently
in my light.

Temptation- Temptation Won

I know that look, he wants me.
What she don't know won't hurt.
He's saying all the right things.
I like the chase.
I'm not turning down an opportunity
to be pleasured, admired and valued.
I can have them both.
Every man I know steps out.
Looking won't hurt.
My body is responding.
What was I suppose to say
no?
I've never said no to the thrill of something new.
I have needs.
He's my type.
My father had multiple women.
polygamy is everywhere these days.
It's just sex.
What if I can't turn it down?
am I selfish?
I don't want to cheat.
but I can't help myself.
I've been this way all my life.
If he won't, he will.
I can't miss out.
There's something better out there.

Is there a guide that teaches us how to manage temptation? There is no way for you to not place yourself in a situation. Temptation is everywhere. Men and woman are stimulated constantly by other individuals by sight, touch, hearing, and even the lure of smell whether we are in a committed relationship or not. We are led by our sexual appetites, instant gratification, addictions, opportunity, and trauma. The desire of the flesh is a spiritual stronghold. I'll even go on to say that without mental restraint, prayer, and discipline, the flesh is untrustworthy. We're not perfect, but God is. We're not perfect, but we do better by doing better.

Sacrifice

When romance is dimmed,
I'll water our union
with the warmth of loyalty.
It will bloom again.
She's so good for me.
I'm flattered, but he's my king.
I have self-control.
We still have our big-engine purr.
My man doesn't deserve betrayal.
She means more to me
than a fling.
Our rapture is worth the sacrifice.
I'm making better decisions.
We're going through a rough patch.
I'm fully aware of the good
with the bad.
I don't know
if I can control myself.
I'll say NO.
I can trust myself.
Everything is not about sex.
I need to heal this part of me.
I love my family.
Pray for deliverance.
"because I can"
is not an excuse.
My boys are going to think
I'm whipped.
My girls can think whatever.
I'll set the example.
Change the narrative.
This is uncommon behavior.
I'm not the man
or woman
I used to be.

Reactive

Who she think she talking to?
She knew what she was doing.
the careless insinuations.
Now that I think about it,
he did that to *provoke me*.
Don't start with me today.
I'll *cuss* you out.
I'm going to do him
how he did me.
He knows how to get
a response from me.
I'll confront her about it.
She thinks I'm stupid,
well, she got *the right one*.
I'll show her I'm not
the *one, three, or five.*
that's odd.
a deliberate whisper.
who are you looking at!
You always starting with me.
it's an extreme obsession.
You go low,
I'll go miserable too.
I don't know any other way.

It can be difficult choosing the high road. You might feel embarrassed, played with, angry, and manipulated at the same time. Ignoring and dismissing is high road techniques. You must practice them and possibly fail the first few attempts. Eventually, with intention and practice, you'll be able to control your emotions. You won't have a desire to react to every action.

Disregard – Ignore - Dismiss

Yes, I'm ignoring you.
I'm not paying you the attention
you crave.
Lord, I need a moment.
I have more to lose.
Let's discuss what's hurting you.
You played with me,
I should play you.
I'm being tested right now.
I really dislike drama.
I'm too calm
and
you can't stand it.
Why you want me angry.
No thanks.
I want you to light.
I've worked hard
for this peace.
I'll pray for you instead.
You go low,
I'll leave you there.
I have zero tolerance
for malicious intent.
I have zero tolerance
for anyone
or anything
that disrupts
my harmony.

Ignorant- Racism & Hate

In my family, this is how it's been.
for generations.
for years.
If my family said it, then it's right.
My race is superior.
My religion is the holiest.
Your history teaches me nothing.
The constitution is inviolable and revered.
Racism doesn't exist.
Hate wears the nation's
best suits.
I dislike rainbow people.
Privilege is acceptable
if it benefits me.
Your race disgusts me.
all of them.
They don't deserve to live.
How does ignorance identify ignorance?
Our historic agendas are a no fail.
The strategy customizes
but the scheme remains the same.
I refuse to acknowledge
your existence and worth,
which ignites your
rage and fury.
The cycle continues.
The narrative continues.
The end.

It's important to address the hidden warfare's in America. Most hate derives from ignorance. We cannot see hate or ignorance if it is not *revealed* or *verbalized*. Turning a blind eye to racism, not acknowledging the real character of America, passing incredulous laws, and not standing for what's right elicits distrust instead of unity. There's just too much information to not have an epiphany at some point. This is a seed to escape the manipulation that has kept us captive.

Appetite for Knowledge

My family's hate
is old as Jim Crow.
Ignorance
benefiting from
darkness.
Been there, didn't like it.
I'm coping to make sense
of the need to
maintain superiority.
I'm exhausting
hateful energy.
The voices of history
are very important.
exposing dark truths
results in accountability.
As I venture into
reading
researching
so much knowledge
contradicts my beliefs.
How would I handle hate?
Looking outside my perspective,
I see a world vastly different.
I think different.
Different isn't threatening!
We need referendums and
constitutional change.
I do not have to be
who I've been.
The more I see,
the more light I seek.
Why again is there a superior race?
Why we can't all survive.
If only we *all* had
a desire to challenge
what we fear
to reveal.

Non-Believer - Why God?

I don't believe in what I can't see.
Hey God, if you're listening,
why would you allow
war
racism
violence
hurricanes
poverty.
Why would you take my child?
You're up there in heaven
looking down *allowing* heartbreak.
Why are children raped or starving?
Do something *if* you're really God.
Are you the same God
that allowed slavery
for hundreds of years.
It's scientifically proven that Genesis 1:1
is scientifically inaccurate.
How can I worship or trust
something I can't see?
Who exactly am I praying to?
They're many gods.
They're many religions.
I provide so I'm God.
I need to understand this
if I'm ever going to believe.
I'm willing to go deep,
but it's not making sense to me.

If you weren't raised in a church, it's possible you've never had a relationship with God. You may have experienced so much pain in your life, you've turned away from God. There are countless reasons to not know God or not believe that God exists. You may not admit it but the more your mind grows, the more you question God. If you travel the world, you're aware of the many different gods, religions, and faiths. I've experienced God and to know God is to be in complete awe with every aspect of life. Most importantly, God's love for us is sufficient even if we're not.

God's Love - Jesus

When I remove my needs
open my heart
in there
I find the reverence of God.
God lives in me.
This is the same God
that created 10,000 species of birds.
The same God
that created the 250,000-pound blue whale
who lives in the magnificent sea
but needs air to breathe.
The Bible introduces God.
His character.
His voice.
His promises.
even the tactics of a fallen angel.
God shows His ultimate love
by forgiving
my sins
my faults
my dark
through the blood.
There's something about the name Jesus.
He is the purest light.
His Will surpasses *all* human understanding.
The Holy Spirit lives in me.
When someone throws
my dark in my face,
I remember God's grace.
I remember how
I kept the faith.
As I get to know Him,
I trust Him to guide my steps.
All that I am
I humbly give
to God.

Jesus loves you so much.

Past

My past broke me.
no love.
Daddy issues
sunk me.
I remember when the innocence
of the world faded.
I remember when I didn't trust
giants.
When I look back at some of my decisions
I understand who I was:
attractively unbalanced
easily influenced
unclothed
a lost soul.
I fought hard not to drown
yet I
yielded to sin.
Blindness guided me
in loops of lust.
independently ignorant.
An abused heart,
trampled
desperate.
My light flickered
a demented life.
conditional loves.
a painful past.

You won't forget. You'll remember what it took to develop real emotions. You had to properly process the light in you others could already see. Cast out the condemnation. Remind your thoughts and your posture that you don't live in the former. You were being shaped and transformed into a wiser you. Make room to grow into who you are meant to be and listen for the voice of God in you.

Future

When I fly over my life
I see my past.
I zoom in on the
suffering,
the difficult moments.
I stop for motivation.
I take off again.
This time elevated
using the pain
to take me
higher than I imagined.
I forgive
my ignorance.
I forgive
the screams
for love
for information
for male attention.
from my inner child.
This time I choose
to stand up
for myself.
The heavy smog
of trauma
and
dark clouds of silence
are gone.
I struggled with the forecast
but I replaced them
with endurance.
God, I need you everyday.
When I fly over my life
I see a miracle.

Infatuate

You're so dam sexy
and attractive.
Thinking about our intimate
exchanges parts oceans.
does it awaken your veins.
I know just what you need
to see me.
to release.
to drown.
oral communication
my best form.
yours too.
compatible.
we talk.
we laugh.
I can't keep my hands off you.
we don't go on dates.
we fulfill aches.
fill in space.
You're a cutie.
You've handed me pleasure.
kissing your way to my
vaginal heart.
I'm screaming
yes, yes, yes
to sweat.
flesh is blinding my judgement
placing me in the palm
of your finger.
When you call,
I cum.
am I foolish?
cause I think
I love you.

Don't be confused.

Love

Those arms
that lift me
also lifts me
in prayer.
covers me
motivates me
and expects nothing in return.
Her mind is her greatest asset.
Our intimacy goes beyond
physical.
the flowers
the safe space
the disagreements
the adventures
the wins
the lows
the investments
the thoughtful lunches
the encouragement
it brings comfort
it brings extreme delight.
You've demonstrated
patterns of love and
unconditional acceptance.
Your face excites my heart.
Your flaws inspire me.
it's your personality.
If I reminisce too much
I'll cry a beloved pain.
The ways you
treat my heart with care
is a selfless form.
my calm.
your storm.
attentive to my silence.
listening to your every word.
Love is captive.
Love freed me.

Phases of Immaturity

Why she let herself get so big.
He's too ugly for me.
I like a bad boy.
my man sells drugs and been to jail.
I steal because I can.
I cheated because it was common.
I didn't speak up,
because I don't care.
it's not my problem.
You can't tell me nothing.
I can take your man.
all men are dogs.
It's okay to lie.
so what if it's wrong.
I find joy in drama.
gossiping with my girls
getting the tea.
not giving a dam.
unfazed and unbothered.
I match hate with hate.
It's about what I can accumulate.
I've always been that pressure.
He was disloyal first.
It's karma.
I didn't ask you.
I know what I'm doing.
I'm real.
I say whatever's
on my mind.

Forgive yourself again and again. Ignorance is a part of the human experience. We learn, then we grow. People experience wicked things before they mature. Only it's not usually spoken testimonials. All the worst things you thought, said, and did, fatefully arrived you at this merciful place. Have compassion to who you were as you promote your new perspectives. As you walk in the light, heal your dark.

Who are you today!

Maturing

What does loving myself
look like?
How do I become
a better version
of me?
Thank God,
I'm not who I used to be.
Deep down,
I know what's right.
This time I choose light.
That flicker of regret
ruptured
a leak for change.
self-evaluation.
self-exploration.
I'll spread love and
unlearn hate.
This is how I grow.
Get close to God
and break the
critical
unkind
envious
unjust
plain ole mean
spirit cycle.
My dark is
only an extension
of my survival.
Their shame
could one day
be my pain.
a counter narrative.
As I heal,
so did my choices.
I choose to confront who I was.
I choose to be the person I needed.
I chose to share wisdom.

Abused

You hurt your biggest supporter
when you balled your fist.
Your face is fear.
You want me to fear you?
You said you loved me.
I can't believe I picked you.
You disguised your tactics
in the name of love.
manipulated my heart.
deceived my mind.
A clever predator you are.
You spoke subliminal languages
to crush my spirit.
A psychological dialect.
the audacity of your ego.
the methods you used to break me, built me.
You said,
"I'm nothing without you."
"I need you."
"No one will treat me like you do."
I hope not.
You might be sorry but
my eye is black.
my lip is busted.
my core is bruised.
my confidence is broken.
How did I get here?

Abuse is never a reflection of who you are or what you did. It's quite the opposite. The abuse reflects the demons inside the abuser. You were skillfully mishandled in an unfair way. Do NOT let anyone steal your dignity. Touch your tears and lift your head up. Recognize when you're in the dark. Leave.
Leave now.

Escape

Dear Lord,
I need you to strengthen me.
what matters most:
loving a dream
or
saving my life?
I will use his deception methods
for my escape.
unhappiness is painted
in my walk.
getting out while I can
frequent my thoughts.
It's clear as each attack
I will no longer
be your punching bag.
I never felt your desire
to change.
I only felt the love
of your pain.
I stayed as long as I could.
To think I felt sorry for you.
Without your cooperation
my love can't heal you.
Your actions translate:
leave now, don't wait.
Before it gets worse
it will get good.
Good luck.
Good riddance.
Goodbye.
God bless.

Stubborn

This is how I'm wired
I can't change.
I don't want to change.
You have a point
but my idea is better.
I was raised to believe
that's wrong
therefore
it's wrong.
I'm not changing my mind.
I know what's best.
I'm not open to your perspective.
call me devil's advocate.
Don't waste your time.
I'm not convinced.
There's no way I'm wrong.
This is how it should go.
I'm not budging.
call it pride.
call it ego.
call it whatever you want.
I'm not really a team player
respectfully.
My way or no way.
I decline.
I disagree.
I don't need an explanation.

Do you have a habit of refusing to comply for no reason? Stubborn has healthy and damaging notes. If you're unable to compromise or participate in a group decision, it might be time to let go, relax, and listen.

Compliant- Let Go

I'm always willing
to learn.
Listening;
a great skill to acquire.
I don't have
all the answers.
I'm willing to hear
all sides.
I've cooperated
in stunting
my ability
to grow.
to see beyond.
I've been stubborn.
He has logical information.
I can compromise.
She has a point.
I'm open to listening.
Knowledge
is infinite.
I'll manage
my strong will.
Let's make the best decision
collectively.
I'll consider that.
I consciously choose
to improve.
I don't have to agree
with you
to hear your perspective.
I'm letting go.
I'm releasing
complete control.

Drug Addiction- Fall Apart Addictions

This is not me.
I lost myself in the high.
I can't stop now if I wanted to.
My family can't know.
I'll disappoint my family.
I can handle the consequences.
I can drink every day.
this is my body.
smoke a lil gas
take a few percs
all in a day's work.
It's medicinal pills.
I need it to cope.
Party all night.
Smoke all day.
I'm stuck to this couch.
Giving myself away to strangers.
I'm caught up in hopeless affection.
lack has control.
I can operate orderly.
this is my life.
I'm falling all
apart.
This is not me.

In these tough moments, it's not easy to acknowledge our self-sabotaging actions. Our habits become addictions in the form of leisure and coping. Since we can still function, we ignore the behavior that prevents us from thinking clearly and accomplishing our goals. The truth is acknowledgement is the starting point to a 180. The hardest part is leaving it behind and maintaining discipline. Right choices take more effort.

Come Back Together - Reform

There's better ways
to manage my anxious mind.
There's better ways
to manage
my time.
connect with courage.
practice discipline.
set boundaries.
Love myself.
I'll try this
over and over
until I get it light.
I'll crush my goals
one by one.
Every day strengthens
my confidence.
I take fight
with each step.
I quit anything that
weakens my mind
forces a mood
corrupts my spirit
harms my body.
As I walk on my way,
the way appears.
My conscious is clear.
I'm proof of working
through your dark.
I'm becoming the best
version of me.
I had to fall apart.
to come back together
refined.

Locked Up - Prison

This is how my family
survives.
I don't want to sell.
I don't want to steal.
I don't want to go to jail.
I'll put money up
just in case.
Serving time
is a badge of honor.
to the streets.
I can bond out.
I knew getting locked up
was a possibility.
a penitentiary chance.
I did what I had to do.
My bail is too high.
No one's answering the phone.
The judge told me I had
one more chance.
I need to get my life together.
I'll get out and move better.
Hustling is all I know.
Nobody *wants* to live
this life, trust me.
To you, it's wrong.
To me, it's a way out.

Free - Freed

All money
isn't worth
the repercussions.
I'm not going back.
There's so much I want to do.
I'm not risking
my freedom.
not anymore.
There must be a better way.
It won't be easy money
but it'll be legit.
I used to hustle, but
I quit.
I'm out now.
I'll show you
a better path.
I didn't have a father figure.
I'm going to be there
to raise my son.
I'm getting a career
to set a positive example.
I'm free.
I'm freed.
I want more
for myself.
better choices.
wiser thoughts.

Assume

why would someone
say it then?
It was headlined
on the news.
The news only report
accurate information.
She been acting funny anyway.
He looked drunk all week.
why don't I just ask?
they all the same.
I don't understand
why they would lie.
The comments said…
Social media said it too.
I'm usually right
about these things.
If it walks like a duck…
It's safe to assume.
I have my sources.
I can draw.
conclusions.
It doesn't take a genius
to figure it out.

In today's world, we have the power to paint narratives with little effort. She said, he said, and the telephone game is the quickest way to digest synthetic information. We live in a world that assumes the worst. Information that's hastily digested without facts or proof. Expand your curiosity and unshackle the constraints placed around cognitive bias mindsets.

Certainty

I can't believe it wasn't true.
Anyone can just say anything.
wow.
the facts were there
the entire time.
I'm not letting the news
control my perceptions.
social media feeds
on dramatical errors.
She wasn't acting funny,
she's battling depression
alone.
He's not an alcoholic,
he's grieving.
He just returned home
from deployment.
They need help.
I should've asked.
I could've helped.
It was easier to assume.
I was wrong.
I didn't consider this…
I didn't know that…
There's more than just
my understanding.
iceberg theory.
I'm learning not to judge.
not to assume.
It could've been me.
Now I know.

Grief – Loss

A piece of my heart
is in the earth.
gone.
I'm crying the memories.
I see you
standing
smiling
talking to me.
I'm collapsing.
I have to remind myself
to breathe
to get up
to eat.
My body's reaction
to a missing heart.
you left me.
How will I survive
the misery?
handle the intensity?
My head is down
I can't look up.
We have so many
things left to do,
now what.
I should've
stayed closer
talked longer
called every day.
I can't measure enough.
Why you, why me.
Why, God?
Grief please don't ruin me.

The Pain

I feel the moments
of heartbreak.
I admit the pain.
I'll allow my body
to respond
to the pain.
This is a new suffering
to my senses.
A mental and emotional
shock.
to lose their existence.
Pain is unapologetic
sometimes.
The feelings of grief
will settle.
I'll find my peace there.
I can manage.
I will manage.
If the suffering revisits,
God is near.
When he refills my
happiness,
I'll feel no guilt.
I clinch the memories
against my eyelids
so I can keep
you close.
Thank you for sharing
your life with me.
Thank you for sharing
your light
with the world.

Perfection

I can't post the picture at the beach
I gained too much weight.
I have the blackest features.
My nose is wide.
My skin is dark.
I'm always good.
They're the perfect couple.
Where is my prince charming?
My family is rachet.
My annual salary is average.
If he's not six feet tall,
I'm not interested.
I like my women
with a tiny waist
and long hair.
I'm 35 and not married.
I'm 40 with no kids.
Who doesn't wear make up?
filters fix the flaws.
If I get a BBL,
he'll stop cheating.
I have mental health conditions,
she won't talk
to a man like me.
I can't show my emotions,
it's weak.
I should look perfect
at all times.

Not Perfect - Authentic

My lips
My birth mark
My skin
My short hair
gives me pure satisfaction.
I'm the most perfect me
I've never seen.
I can communicate my feelings.
If I don't lose weight
it's mine to keep.
You see rachet,
I see struggle.
You see grit,
I see character.
I'm not a tomboy in a dress
I'm me.
Thank you for identifying
my royal features.
I don't need make-up
I wear it.
He's cheating himself.
I'm worthy unmarried.
I'm worthy with no kids.
I support you
no matter what.
I'm here for you.
I fit in perfectly
where I am appreciated.

Don't get caught up in the fantasy of perfection. The fake perception of reality we see and hear contradicts the reality we live day-to-day. There is no such thing as perfection. Show up authentic instead.

Goliath

I'm more powerful.
It's impossible.
This fight you will not win.
zero possibility.
I have numbers.
I have many men.
it's concerning you think
otherwise.
I know you're scared.
I'll make you fight.
I'll defeat you
mentally.
I've been watching.
I've been listening.
secretly.
May the Lord be with you.
There are no rules
in an attack.
This will be another defeat.
I'm the champion.
Tell your God
he's not real.

David

I will risk it all
in the name of the Father.
A long prep of courage.
I can do anything
through Christ
that gives me strength.*
I am one of His
strongest
hardworking
resilient
Soldiers.
How bad do I want it?
real bad.
the victory isn't mine,
God wins.
arrogance is
unnecessary.
It's a matter of
life or death.
I choose a lifetime.
I'm soaked in
God's grace.
listening for
God's wisdom.
The real fight
is internal.
His love for me
is eternal.

The story of David and Goliath: 1 Samuel 17.

Philippians 4:13 (TCW)

Cocky

I get attention
everywhere I go.
not my homegirls
me.
I'm the baddie.
I don't need help
from you or
anyone.
I can get another you
easily.
This face card has
no spending limit.
I'm the best
you'll ever have.
I get what I want
when I want.
I appreciate the compliment
but I know
I look good.
He'd never cheat on me.
I'm cuter than you.
I'm out your league.
You do what for a living?
baby I can't hear you.
You should be happy
I chose you.
I'm not cocky,
I'm confident.

Cockiness lacks humility. When you have an excessive opinion about yourself, you cross the thin line between cocky and confident. Self-confidence with a humble approach gives off a "light" heart.

Confident

God favored me.
I am more than
pretty.
It took a long time
to love myself.
I didn't love
the beauty you see
right away.
I'm physically
and mentally
attractive.
I thought looks were
all there was to me.
Thank you for the compliment.
I'm blessed.
I don't look like
what I've been through.
I'm not as beautiful
as my spirit.
I don't need
to compare
myself to anyone
but me.
I'm classic.
I'm elegant.
I like words of affirmation.
reassurance.
I have flaws like everyone else.
I'm certain I'm the best candidate.
I'm confident in my abilities.
I'm the best me.

MOON WALK

and - THE DUALITIES

While you're on the path of self-exploration – the purpose of better understanding yourself – you'll face the darkest parts of yourself. We operate in the darkness more times than we realize and, in many cases, it's dark versus light. Yet, at times it's dark *and* light, coexisting in the dualities.

The Dualities.

Here's a very clear perspective: we're only human. A little bit of this and a little bit of that. While we're walking towards the light, we're healing. There is no space to condemn, only a space to just *be*.

Due to various life situations, we've had to survive this way... combinations tangled on the pendulum of darkness *and* light. The next pages focus more on the *"and"*.

Depressed

What day is it?
"Another day of pretending"
Everyone loves me
so why do I feel alone.
I feel like I'm two different people;
the life of the party and
the epitome of sadness.
a self-pity party.
Darkness has
swallowed me.
I have no appetite for life.
The person I love
don't love me.
No one hears the gloom
in my eyes.
No one sees my panicking
thoughts.
My mind is in control
below zero hope.
Erasing my existence
triggers clarity.
I have no appetite.
I'm easily disguised
in a dimension
of superficial smiles.
My face under the mask
low-spirited.
sad.

Laughter

I love laughter.
I enjoy putting a smile on your face.
It makes me feel connected
to something
to someone.
It's the only thing I have left to give.
I have a skillful purpose:
to act normal.
to perform happy.
to evoke happiness.
I smile.
even if it's not real.
Have you noticed
a smile
can swiftly pass?
To see the joy on a kid's face,
my inner child escapes.
Laughter cures the soul
but it's brief.
A glimmer of happy spirits.
A fleeting home of raised
cheekbones.
Making the world laugh
is an art form.

When we laugh, are we happy? It's not as simple as it seems is it. We can conclude that it's possible to live in a depressed state of mind by masking our feelings with laughter. Acknowledge the pain. But please remove the depression out of your life. It's easier said than believed. It seems we give to others what *we* really need. Love. Appreciation. Loyalty. Attention. Time. Light.

Laughter is a great place to visit. Find your joy.

Empty

Who am I doing it for?
the fans.
the nay sayers.
I have something to prove.
Attention feeds
my confidence.
When it's just me,
I feel worthless.
a numbing emptiness.
Isolation is a
desolate wilderness.
If I'm not showing it off
I have no purpose.
my empty thoughts.
Who am I
without
things
titles
or recognition?
No amount of applause
fills the void.
I feel disconnected.
With all the luxuries
I still feel abandoned.
Maybe I need passion
and love.
a masquerade.
hollow masked.
Dressed in
conflicted layers.

Have It All Together

Business is booming.
Celebrated my birthday
with a lit party.
My kids are loved and
want for nothing.
I'm planning another vacation.
I received a promotion.
This week is my wedding anniversary.
I paid off my house.
I have my doctorate.
My credit score is higher this month.
Life is great.
My plants are thriving.
I have a new girlfriend.
My boyfriend proposed.
I have over 30,000 followers.
I have two job offers.
I'm starting another business.
I have a lot of friends.
I brought a new car.
I'm wealthy with many assets.

This is an intriguing combination. Unsurprisingly, social media is the gateway for blurred motives. The quickest way to blur your motive is to seek gratification from likes or from others. Be clear of your motivation. Be sure everything you seek externally is resolved internally.

Follower

I followed.
Before I led,
I had to learn
how to follow.
A great follower
finds their own
style of leading.
As a leader,
I'm a follower.
I still have a boss.
A leader shows
future leaders
how to lead,
but
most importantly
how to overcome
if they fail.
How to receive respect
without asking
and
how to give respect
even if it's not earned.
That's the
military life,
follow the person in front.
follow the leader.

Leader

I'm in the front
leading the way.
They're listening
all the while
calculating what I say
watching what I do
and what I don't do.
Taking care of others
is a major responsibility.
when your heart is in it.
gathering information.
sharing wisdom.
giving them alternatives.
motivating them.
keeping them on track.
all the while still learning.
showing them
the light
in the dark.
my resilient talk.
humbling myself.
offering my flaws.
providing an
escape from
dark mindsets.
A living example.
growing daily yet
leading well.

How did I learn how to be an authentic leader? by following, growing my skills, and leading from the heart.

No

no.
no.
no.
no.
no.
no.
no.
no.
no.
no.
no.
no.
no.
no.
no.
no.
no.
No.

The answer is no.

No

No, I need time.
No, I'm still healing.
No, I'm socially drained.
No, I'm tired.
No, it's not a safe space.
No, I have other plans.
No, that no longer excites me.
No, that's not the best choice for me.
No, I'm mentally exhausted.
No, that's messy.
No, I'm protecting my energy.
No, I have a bad feeling.
No, I'm focused.
No, I rather not entertain negativity.
No, thank you.
No, thanks.

We can be kind and still say "no". The world may associate no with disagreeable or selfish, but perhaps saying "no" is a "yes" in your best interest. Answering no is more self-polite than answering yes at the expense of your yourself.

Trauma

I don't trust myself
to make the
right decision.
The mental baggage
gets heavy.
I'll never get over this.
I have trust issues.
I've failed before.
I don't have anymore
fight left.
I have no more strength.
Thinking about trying
stresses me out.
I have anxiety now.
I've been through hell
twice.
places of war.
I've been taken
advantage of.
the past depresses me.
I have trust issues.
I'm afraid to get help.
I'm struggling
to be positive.
I'm afraid to admit
I'm traumatized.
I don't know
if I can get
through this.

Progress

I can do it.
I can do this.
One step at a time.
but what if I fail. å
what if I don't.
There're no other options.
I owe it to myself to try.
Yes, I did it!
Yes, I got the job!
Yes, I can do it!
Thank God I passed.
This is a step forward.
This is the ultimate lesson
of survival.
I'm resilient.
I'll never give up.
Get back up.
Get up!
I'm broken,
but I can't quit.

Cry yourself to sleep and wake up! Trauma can also strengthen you. Wake up renewed and ready to begin again and again.
If you have to.

Mind

Pray.
A crowded rolodex of thoughts
past
present
future.
Occupying space
with the day-to-day tasks.
things to do.
what ifs.
why comes.
and how to's.
Tribulations to
hurdle and
duties to fulfill.
devious influences.
choices.
stress.
overthinking.
Wrong thoughts
venture in.
I cast them out.
That win got to my head.
I struggle to find
vacancy with
the business of life
disappointment
and excitement.
The listener.
absorbing the trials of others.
The Encourager.
holding on.
Balancing my conscious.

Heart

The heart.
My courage.
My spirit.
My soul.
Passion lives
in the rhythm.
That loss
won't live
in my
heart.
I should place
7 guards
to filter
the fraud
the wickedness
the lies
full-time.
I chose God.
a real love,
Guarding the Gates.
No need for
an evil eye.
He purifies
my tainted heart
aligns my soul.
The Word
arms me with a
powerful heart.
no vacancy for
heart aches
or
heart breaks.

Confused

So much is happening
in life,
I don't know what
to decide.
Am I ready for another child?
Should I pursue a new career or
stay with this company
for another 10 years?
I think it's time I did
something for me.
We'll have to relocate.
My family won't be thrilled.
I'll be turning down
a promotion.
I'll have to sell the house.
I should be married by now.
My spouse loves me,
but he's not in love
anymore.
I'm almost 40,
how should I dress?
Should I go to
graduate school?
The housing market
is extremely high.
Should I rent or
purchase a house?
Where do I want to live?
I have a law degree but
I want to pursue
my culinary dreams.
How do I know I'm
living my purpose?

Grateful

difficulties
problems
decisions
create opportunities.
opportunities to learn.
opportunities to grow.
I'm grateful for my family.
I'm grateful for my child.
I'm grateful for my career.
I'm grateful for the option to relocate.
I grateful for money in my bank account.
I'm grateful for old age.
I'm grateful for a new chapter.
I'm grateful for a new home.
I'm grateful for my discernment.
I'm grateful for the detour.
I'm grateful for my talent.
I'm grateful for the ability to decide.
I'm grateful for being bold.
I'm grateful for the strength it takes to be alive.
I'm grateful I'm in my right mind.
I'm grateful for the blessings I receive.
I'm grateful for the dilemmas.
I'm grateful for the suffering.
I'm grateful for reflection.
I'm grateful for the next step in my journey.
I'm grateful that moment didn't kill me.

Gratitude is a light perspective. Confusion will easily run you into a hole of darkness. A grateful heart keeps you grounded and aware.

STEM

Science
Technology
Engineering
Math
Solving number equations
come easy to me.
As a child
I loved Legos.
I like biology.
I built my computer.
Space amazes me.
I started an application.
I want to build houses.
I want to go to the moon.
I memorized the Periodic Table.
I manage money well.
I can build anything with
pieces of wood.
I enjoy creating websites.
Numbers excite me.
I specialize in clinical research.
I'm an electrician.
I want to be an astronaut.
I develop software.
I want to go to the moon.
How does environmental engineer sound?
I like the sound of an ESPN statistician.

ARTS

Words intrigue me.
I have an eye for design.
Colors are hypnotizing.
Pottery calms me.
I draw portraits.
I'm a makeup artist.
I love to paint.
I want to help children cope with life.
I want to write a book.
I have natural creative skills.
I'm a glass sculptor.
I'm a theater major.
I taught myself how to
play the guitar.
I can read music.
I love the piano.
I won numerous spelling bees.
I'm an editor.
I'm in performing arts.
I want to be a photographer.
I specialize in digital arts.
I love fashion.
I want to be a communications officer.
I enjoy counseling.
I like the sound of librarian.

We're not only STEM or only ARTS. We are complex and eclectic in our thoughts, personalities, and careers. We excel at more than one thing on both ends of the spectrum. It's okay and very common. Shine your light in everything you desire.

Different – by Society

I have pink eyes and blond hair.
I have PTSD.
I'm not loud or interested in others.
I'm a 30-year-old virgin.
I don't sleep around.
I'm gay.
I don't identify as male or female.
My hair is coily.
I'm adult at 4 ft, 6 inches.
I'm super thin.
My skin is dark.
I'm extremely shy.
I feel things deeply.
I like to eat.
I lost my hair.
I feel overwhelmed in crowds.
I like being with myself a lot.
I'm a large man.
I pray often.
I can talk to anybody.
I've changed.
I don't eat eggs, milk, or fish.
I'm a big girl.
I know what I want.
I speak my mind.

.

I am – I'm

I'm albino.
I'm a veteran.
I'm an introvert.
I have a devout relationship with God.
I respect my body.
I'm a member of the LGBTIQA+ community.
I'm a member of the LGBTIQA+ community.
I'm black, an African American.
I'm a person, a little person.
I'm a model.
I'm black, an African American.
I'm socially awkward.
I'm hypersensitive.
I'm a foodie.
I'm bald.
I have anxiety.
I enjoy my solitude.
This is my body.
I love God.
I'm an extrovert.
I'm growing.
I'm vegan.
This is my body.
I'm assertive.
I'm confident.

At times, we may have to stand alone because we may look or act different. Stand!

Night

dark.
My pupils are black
in the most silent moments.
I uncuff
the impulses that
drive darkness.
a choice.
a fed attack.
Darkness unsolicited
surrounds me.
An easy left turn
onto deaf ears,
into controlled evils,
by organized demons.
I'm cuffed
blinded
on a roundabout.
blinded in
the valley of life.
I can't see
in the dark.
a mental destruction.
I'm so far gone
too far lost.
Light,
can you
find me
in the darkness?

Moon

I see the right.
I'm using my moon,
I see the light.
Proudly fighting
for my life.
for my salvation.
I'm a traitor of the night.
Using the light as adrenaline
to walk in the night.
Next time I fall in a fight,
I'll stand up
badly bruised
facing the light.
I survived the night.
I found the light.
I can see clearly.
I can see at night.

Darkness can motivate or discourage you, grow or shrink you, destroy or enlighten you.

Which will you decide?

Our choices have a huge bearing on who we become. These are my answers for all of it, most of it. My grit, my viewpoint, my thoughts, and processes to innerstand and overcome the evolution of life. I learned to deal with the principalities of darkness with an abundance of light. I don't mean to drown the truth by being too optimistic but, we *need* an excess of light. Non-negotiable. While you're on your moon walk, don't forget to see the beauty in the lessons. Stay connected to your light. It will take you forward determinedly!

MOON WALK

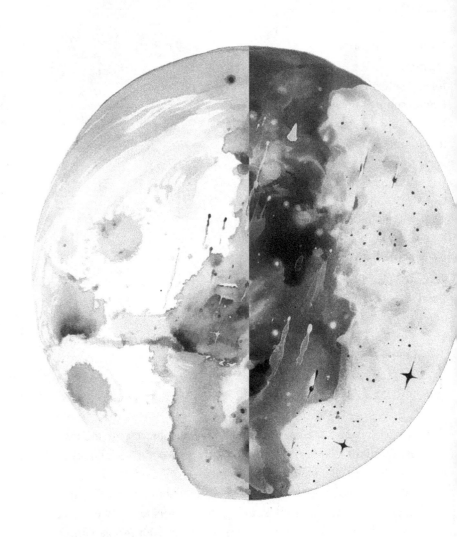

ACKNOWLEDGEMENTS

MOST OF ALL, thank you Jesus from the bottom of my heart. You've been holding my hand since I was that vibrant, curious, and rebellious little girl. You knew what it will take to get me here and for that, I give you all the praise. I'm grateful for your light in my life.

My man, thank you to my man. Mo, you are the center of my universe. I appreciate your gentle tolerance of me: my overly affectionate ways and my constant observations. Thank you for always supporting me. I adore you.

Mom & Dad, thank you for being my parents and for always believing in me. Ma, I can feel your strength in my veins. My creative queen, I am because of who you are. Thank you for birthing me.

My birth father, Quincy. I miss you. Thank you for bringing me into this world.

Grandma, one of the most generous women I know. Your wisdom was instrumental to my beginnings. I feel your presence every time I pray. Thank you for covering me.

Grandaddy, my grandaddy! I miss you. Thank you for the example.

My sister, Daniell. You're so special and I hope you never forget that. Your love is raw, loud, and selfless. My (insert middle name). Thank you for loving your big sister.

My besties, Laina and Cat. Your friendships are irreplaceable. Thank you for seeing me and still loving me.

My birthday twin, Khaleelah. You're one of a kind. Thank you for your loyalty.

To my nieces, nephews, cousins, aunts, uncles, extended family, and anyone that has inspired me, *thank you for being a part of my journey.*

Printed in the USA
CPSIA information can be obtained
at www.ICGtesting.com
LVHW081739021123
762795LV00002B/3